Developing Numeracy

USING AND APPLYING MATHS

INVESTIGATIONS FOR THE DAILY MATHS LESSON

year

Hilary Koll and Steve Mills

A & C BLACK

D1078967

Mathematical skills and processes

Page	Activity title	Predict	Visualise	Look for pattern	Record	Reason	Make decisions	Estimate	Explain	Be systematic	Co-operate	Compare	Test ideas	Trial and improvement	Ask own questions	Generalise	Check	Simplify
	Numbers and the number system																	
14	Take the challenge	○			○	○				●		○	○	●				
15	Money matters	●			○					●			○				○	
16	Printing patterns	○	○	●		○			○							●		
17	Mind reading						●	○		●			○				○	○
18	Hair wash calendar	●		○	○	●			○			○					○	
	Calculations																	
19	Tea-time for Toby	○		○	○	○			○	●		○	○			●	○	
20	Split decisions	○		●	○	○			○			○	○					
21	Pattern codes		○	●		○	○							○				
22	Bedroom makeover		●		○	○	●	○									○	
23	Earring designs				○	●	●	○				○	○	○				
24	Machine magic	○		●		●	○						○					
25	Multiplying mayhem	●		○	○				○	●	○	○						
26	Wheel patterns		○	●		○						●					○	
27	Remainder patterns	●		●	○	○							●			○		
28	Discuss it				○	●			●		●		○					○
	Solving problems																	
29	Triple dominoes		○	○	○					●		●					●	
30	Shooting star	○		●		○						○	○			●		
31	Make way		○			○	●		○				○		○			
32	Big Wheel challenge: 1		●	○	○					●		○	○			○		
33	Big Wheel challenge: 2		○	●	○							○	○				●	
34	Combination locks		○				●			●		○	○			○		
	Handling data																	
35	New school furniture				○		●				●				○			○
36	Pet prizes	○			●				○			○	○			○		●
	Measures, shape and space																	
37–38	Extra square: 1 and 2		●	○	●					○		○	○	●			○	○
39	It's all in the shape		○		○				●		●	●	○					
40	Clock angles		●		○					●	●	○						
41	Point patterns			●		○			●				○			○		
42	Star gazing	○	●	○		○		○					○			●		
43	Ribbon predictions	●	●									○	●					
44	Starman		○		●	○							○					
45–46	Tile tricks: 1 and 2	○	●	●	○		●					○				○		
47	Exercise mats		●	○	○					●		○					○	
48	Spiralling out of control	○				○	●				●		○				○	

● Key processes identified on the activity sheet ○ Additional processes involved in the activity

2

Contents

Mathematical skills and processes   2

Introduction   5–6

Notes on the activities   7–13

Numbers and the number system

Take the challenge	reading and writing whole numbers in figures and words	14
Money matters	ordering amounts of money, using £.p notation	15
Printing patterns	describing and extending number sequences	16
Mind reading	ordering a set of whole numbers	17
Hair wash calendar	recognising and using multiples up to the tenth multiple and beyond	18

Calculations

Tea-time for Toby	consolidating addition facts for small numbers	19
Split decisions	using known number facts and place value to add numbers	20
Pattern codes	using known number facts and place value to add numbers	21
Bedroom makeover	using known number facts and place value to add numbers	22
Earring designs	using known number facts and place value to add numbers	23
Machine magic	using understanding of multiplication and division, and their relationship to addition and subtraction	24
Multiplying mayhem	knowing by heart multiplication facts for all tables to 10	25
Wheel patterns	knowing by heart multiplication facts for all tables to 10	26
Remainder patterns	finding remainders after division	27
Discuss it	using known number facts and place value to solve problems	28

Solving problems

Triple dominoes	solving mathematical problems or puzzles; recognising patterns	29
Shooting star	solving mathematical problems or puzzles; recognising patterns	30
Make way	solving mathematical problems or puzzles; explaining reasoning	31
Big Wheel challenge: 1 and 2	solving mathematical problems or puzzles; recognising patterns	32–33
Combination locks	solving mathematical problems or puzzles; suggesting extensions	34

Handling data

New school furniture	collecting, organising and representing data	35
Pet prizes	collecting, organising and representing data	36

Measures, shape and space

Extra square: 1 and 2	visualising 2-D shapes and patterns; beginning to understand area	37–38
It's all in the shape	visualising and describing 2-D shapes and patterns	39
Clock angles	knowing that a quarter turn is 90° or a right angle	40
Point patterns	recognising positions and directions on a co-ordinate grid	41

Star gazing	visualising 2-D shapes and patterns	42
Ribbon predictions	identifying nets of simple solid shapes	43
Starman	describing positions and directions	44
Tile tricks: 1 and 2	making patterns and discussing properties such as lines of symmetry	45–46
Exercise mats	visualising 2-D shapes and patterns	47
Spiralling out of control	estimating and measuring lines to the nearest half centimetre	48

Published 2005 by A & C Black Publishers Limited
37 Soho Square, London W1D 3QZ
www.acblack.com

ISBN-10: 0-7136-7139-4
ISBN-13: 978-0-7136-7139-1

Copyright text © Hilary Koll and Steve Mills, 2005
Copyright illustrations © David Benham, 2005
Copyright cover illustration © Charlotte Hard, 2005
Editors: Lynne Williamson and Marie Lister
Designer: Heather Billin

The authors and publishers would like to thank Jane McNeill and Catherine Yemm for their advice in producing this series of books.

A CIP catalogue record for this book is available from the British Library.

Printed in and bound in Great Britain by Cromwell Press Ltd, Trowbridge, Wiltshire.

A & C Black uses paper produced with elemental chlorine-free pulp, harvested from managed sustainable forests.

Introduction

Developing Numeracy: Using and Applying Maths is a series of seven photocopiable activity books designed to be used during the daily maths lesson. The books focus on using and applying mathematics, as referred to in the National Numeracy Strategy *Framework for teaching mathematics*. The activities are intended to be used in the time allocated to pupil activities during the main part of the lesson. They are designed to develop and reinforce the skills and processes that are vital to help children use and apply their maths.

Using and applying mathematics

There are several different components which make up the **content** of maths and form the bulk of any maths curriculum:

- **mathematical facts**, for example, a triangle has three sides;
- **mathematical skills**, such as counting;
- **mathematical concepts**, like place value.

For maths teaching to be successful, it is vital that children can *use* this mathematical content beyond their classroom, either in real-life situations or as a basis for further understanding. However, in order to do so, they require extra abilities over and above the mathematical content they have learned. These extra abilities are often referred to as the **processes** of mathematical activity. It is these processes which make mathematical content usable.

As an example, consider this question:
How many triangles are there in this shape?

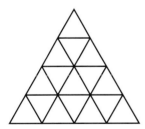

The mathematical content required is only:
- the **fact** that a triangle has three sides;
- the **skill** of counting.

As such, it could be expected that very young children could solve this problem. The fact that they cannot suggests that other abilities are involved. These are the processes, and for this question they include:

- visualising the different-sized triangles;
- being systematic in counting all the triangles of different sizes;
- looking for patterns in the numbers of triangles;
- trial and improvement;
- recording.

Unless children can apply these processes in this situation, then however good their counting skills and knowledge of triangles may be, they will fail.

The 'solving problems' strand of the *Framework for teaching mathematics* emphasises the importance of using and applying mathematics. This series of books is intended to make explicit the skills and processes involved in learning how to put maths knowledge to use.

Using and Applying Maths Year 4 supports the development of the using and applying processes by providing opportunities to introduce and practise them through a series of activities. On the whole these activities are designed for children to work on independently, although this is not always possible and occasionally some children may need support.

Pre-school children are naturally inquisitive about the world around them. They love to explore and experiment, and to make marks and record things on paper in their own idiosyncratic ways. Unfortunately, once at school the focus is often placed firmly on the maths content alone and children can be led to believe that maths is not a subject of exploration, but rather one of simply learning the 'right way to do things'. As a result, when older children are asked to explore and investigate maths they are often at a loss if their maths teaching to date has not encouraged and built upon their natural instincts.

Year 4 helps children to develop the following processes:

- predicting
- visualising
- looking for pattern
- recording
- reasoning
- making decisions
- estimating
- explaining
- being systematic
- co-operating
- comparing
- testing ideas
- trial and improvement
- asking own questions
- generalising
- checking
- simplifying

When using these activities, the focus need not be on the actual mathematical content. Instead, the teacher's demonstrations, discussions and questioning should emphasise the processes the children are using. A summary of the skills and processes covered by each activity is shown on page 2. When appropriate, invite the children to explain their thinking to others. Research has shown that children develop processes most successfully when the teacher encourages them to act as experts rather than novices, allowing them to work autonomously and encouraging a range of approaches to any problem rather than constraining discussion to produce an overall class plan. The children should evaluate their own plans against other plans in the posing, planning and monitoring phases of the lessons.

Extension

Many of the activity sheets end with a challenge (**Now try this!**) which reinforces and extends the children's learning, and provides the teacher with an opportunity for assessment. On occasion, it may be helpful to read the instructions  with the children before they begin the activity. For some of the challenges the children will need to record their answers on a separate piece of paper.

Organisation

Very little equipment is needed, but it will be useful to have the following resources available: coloured pencils, counters, scissors, coins, squared paper, hundred squares, number lines and number tracks.

To help teachers select appropriate learning experiences for the children, the activities are grouped into sections within the book. However, the activities are not expected to be used in this order unless stated otherwise. The sheets are intended to support, rather than direct, the teacher's planning.

Some activities can be made easier or more challenging by masking or substituting numbers. You may wish to re-use pages by copying them onto card and laminating them.

Teachers' notes

Brief notes are provided at the foot of each page giving ideas and suggestions for maximising the effectiveness of the activity sheets. These can be masked before copying.

Solutions and further explanations of the activities can be found on pages 7–13, together with examples of questions that you can ask.

Whole class warm-up activities

The following activities provide some practical ideas which can be used to introduce the main teaching part of the lesson.

Reasoning

Choose a number between 1 and 100. Challenge the class to find out which number it is by asking questions such as *Is it a multiple of 5?* Praise questions that narrow down the field significantly: for example, *Is it odd? Is it below 25? Is it a multiple of three?* Encourage the children to work systematically towards the answer, and discourage wild guesses.

Being systematic

Draw a T-shirt, trousers and a hat on the board. Explain that you can have red or yellow clothes and ask the children to suggest how someone could be dressed: for example, in a red hat, a yellow T-shirt and red trousers. Working with the children's suggestions, draw each of the eight combinations on the board, asking questions such as: *How many hats have we drawn? How many yellow clothes have we drawn? Are we missing any?* Extend the activity by including an additional item of clothing, such as a scarf, in each of the two colours.

Co-operating and making decisions

Write a number statement on the board, such as $30 \div 5 = 6$. Ask the children, working in pairs, to make up a story to match the statement: for example, *Thirty children played football in the Games lesson. Each team had five players and there were six teams.* Ask the class to decide which was the most interesting story.

Visualising

Draw a shape or letter on a sheet of paper, deciding on its size, orientation and position on the paper, for example:

Without showing the paper to the children, describe what you have drawn: for example, *On a portrait piece of paper I have drawn a capital 'B' in the top right-hand corner. The 'B' is the right way up and fills nearly a quarter of the sheet.* Ask the children to recreate your drawing on their own sheet of paper.

Numbers and the number system

Take the challenge (page 14)

☆ *Processes: trial and improvement, be systematic, predict, reason, test ideas, record, compare*

The largest even number that can be made is 8970 (BAN). The word with a number closest to 5000 is LAND (4971).

There are many words which give numbers between 800 and 3000. Examples include AND (971), ANT (978), MEN (2370), MEND (2371), MET (2308), MAD (2901), MAT (2908), MAN (2970).

Large differences between two words with one letter changed include MEND and BEND with a difference of 6000.

Suggested questions:

- How could you show this on a poster?
- What other questions could you ask?

Money matters (page 15)

☆ *Processes: predict, be systematic, test ideas, record, check*

There are 24 possible amounts:

Coins	Notes		
	£5	£10	£20
1p	£5.03	£10.03	£20.03
2p	£5.06	£10.06	£20.06
5p	£5.15	£10.15	£20.15
10p	£5.30	£10.30	£20.30
20p	£5.60	£10.60	£20.60
50p	£6.50	£11.50	£21.50
£1	£8.00	£13.00	£23.00
£2	£11.00	£16.00	£26.00

Encourage the children to work systematically and to compare solutions to see how they are organised and which is easiest to follow.

Suggested questions:

- Why did you predict that?
- How close was your prediction?
- Are you sure you have found all the possible amounts?
- How does the table help you to see the results?

Printing patterns (page 16)

☆ *Processes: look for pattern, generalise, visualise, predict, reason, explain*

The solutions are as follows:

triangle	1	7	13	19	25	31	37	43	49	55
square	2	8	14	20	26	32	38	44	50	56
pentagon	3	9	15	21	27	33	39	45	51	57
hexagon	4	10	16	22	28	34	40	46	52	58
heptagon	5	11	17	23	29	35	41	47	53	59
octagon	6	12	18	24	30	36	42	48	54	60

Note that the position numbers of octagons are multiples of 6, pentagons are odd multiples of 3, all shapes with even numbers of sides are in even positions, and all shapes with odd numbers of sides are in odd positions. Patterns in the units digits can also be explored.

Suggested questions/prompts:

- What patterns do you notice?
- Which shape will be in position number 72/81?
- Tell me a position number where a triangle will appear.

Mind reading (page 17)

☆ *Processes: be systematic, reason, estimate, generalise, check, test ideas*

There are 21 possible numbers:

105	114	123	132	141	150
204	213	222	231	240	
303	312	321	330		
402	411	420			
501	510				
600					

Numbers from 100 to 400:	15	(Now try this! 26)
Numbers from 401 to 700:	6	(Now try this! 24)
Numbers above 700:	0	(Now try this! 15)

Suggested questions:

- Can you use the digit 8 in any of the numbers?
- Why do you think more solutions lie in this group of numbers?
- How do you know that you have found all the numbers?

Hair wash calendar (page 18)

☆ *Processes: reason, predict, look for pattern, explain, compare, record, check*

The solutions are as follows:

No. of children	Dates
1	1st, 7th, 11th, 13th, 17th, 19th, 23rd, 29th, 31st
2	2nd, 3rd, 5th, 9th, 14th, 21st, 22nd, 25th, 26th, 27th
3	4th, 8th, 10th, 15th, 16th, 28th
4	6th, 18th, 20th
5	12th, 24th, 30th

The date when all six children wash their hair will be 1st March in a normal year and 29th February in a leap year. This is the 60th day of the year (60 is the first multiple of 1, 2, 3, 4, 5 and 6). More confident children could explore the implications if there were seven children. The first multiple of the numbers 1 to 7 is 420 – which would be 24th February the following year (assuming 365 days).

Other patterns include the following: the dates when only one hair wash takes place are odd (and also prime); all the dates when four and five washes take place are even; all the dates when five washes take place are multiples of 6 (12, 24 and 30).

Questions can be asked about the information gathered to help the children see the importance of recording carefully.

- On which three consecutive dates in January do only two hair washes take place?
- Who didn't wash their hair on 12th/15th/20th January?
- What patterns have you found?

Calculations

Tea-time for Toby (page 19)

☆ *Processes: be systematic, generalise, compare, check, record, look for pattern, reason, predict, test ideas, explain*

Solutions are as follows:

Number of steps	Number of different ways
1	1
2	2
3	4
4	8
5	16
6	32

Thus seven steps will have 64 ways and eight steps will have 128 ways.

The ways of climbing five steps and six steps are given below.

Five steps (16 ways):
1 + 1 + 1 + 1 + 1,
1 + 1 + 1 + 2, 1 + 1 + 2 + 1, 1 + 2 + 1 + 1, 2 + 1 + 1 + 1,
1 + 1 + 3, 1 + 3 + 1, 3 + 1 + 1,
1 + 4, 4 + 1,
1 + 2 + 2, 2 + 1 + 2, 2 + 2 + 1,
2 + 3, 3 + 2,
5

Six steps (32 ways):
1 + 1 + 1 + 1 + 1 + 1,
1 + 1 + 1 + 1 + 2, 1 + 1 + 1 + 2 + 1, 1 + 1 + 2 + 1 + 1,
1 + 2 + 1 + 1 + 1, 2 + 1 + 1 + 1 + 1,
1 + 1 + 1 + 3, 1 + 1 + 3 + 1, 1 + 3 + 1 + 1, 3 + 1 + 1 + 1,
1 + 1 + 4, 1 + 4 + 1, 4 + 1 + 1,
1 + 5, 5 + 1,
1 + 1 + 2 + 2, 1 + 2 + 1 + 2, 1 + 2 + 2 + 1, 2 + 2 + 1 + 1,
2 + 1 + 2 + 1, 2 + 1 + 1 + 2,
1 + 2 + 3, 1 + 3 + 2, 2 + 1 + 3, 3 + 1 + 2, 2 + 3 + 1,
3 + 2 + 1,
2 + 2 + 2,
3 + 3,
2 + 4, 4 + 2,
6

Encourage the children to compare solutions, and collectively write a class list. The children should explain the strategies they used to help them find the solutions: for example, 'I moved the group of four steps to each possible position in the set of numbers'; 'For six steps I used the answers to five steps, writing out all the five-step solutions with '1 +' in front of them.'

Suggested questions/prompts:
- Could you do the same steps but in a different order?
- Do you notice any patterns? Explain them.
- What strategies did you use?

Split decisions (page 20)

☆ *Processes: look for pattern, reason, predict, test ideas, compare, record, explain*

For the digits to give the same answers, the second digit must be the total of the first and third digits. The fourth digit can be any digit at all, for example:

35 + 20 = 55   35 + 28 = 63
3 + 52 + 0 = 55   3 + 52 + 8 = 63

In the sets of digits on the activity sheet, the second, third and fourth sets of digits work in this way.

Suggested questions/prompts:
- What do you think might make some sets of digits give the same answers and others not?
- What have you noticed about the second digit?
- Change one of the digits. Does it still work?

Pattern codes (page 21)

☆ *Processes: look for pattern, visualise, reason, make decisions, trial and improvement*

As a further extension, the children could make pattern codes with a total of 100 in different ways. Some examples are shown below.

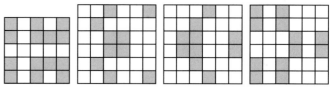

The children could make a poster compiling all the different '100' solutions they find. Once one solution has been found, they can explore ways of exchanging squares: for example, exchanging two 2s for four 1s, or two 32s for four 16s.

Suggested questions:
- What have you discovered?
- Are all your patterns symmetrical?
- Can you find any pattern codes with a total of 100?
- Now you have found one solution, what could you do to find more?

Bedroom makeover (page 22)

☆ *Processes: make decisions, visualise, record, estimate, reason, check*

Encourage careful recording and ask the children to explain to others in the class why they made the choices they did. Once they have completed their choices, they could draw a plan or picture of the bedroom as they imagine it will be.

Suggested questions:
- Why did you choose that item?
- Was it your first choice?
- Did you have to alter any of your choices? Why?

Earring designs (page 23)

☆ *Processes: make decisions, reason, record, estimate, compare, trial and improvement, test ideas*

The cost of the given earrings are £1.15, £1.35, £2.05 and £2.50. The following are example solutions to the second question:

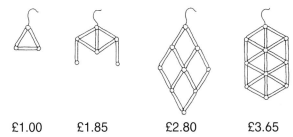

£1.00   £1.85   £2.80   £3.65

For the extension activity, the children should find that it is not possible to make an earring costing 80p unless two beads can be placed directly next to each other (making an earring with one piece of wire, one hook and three beads).

Suggested questions:
- What did you notice about the number of beads when the total was an even/odd amount?
- Why do you think this is?
- What rules could we make about what the earring must look like?
- How much would a pair of these earrings cost?

Machine magic (page 24)
☆ *Processes: reason, look for pattern, test ideas, predict, make decisions*

The number subtracted is always a multiple of the input number and it is also a multiple of the number one less than the multiplying number. So, if the input number is 6 and the multiplying number is 3, the number to be subtracted is 12 (6 × 2). Encourage children who find the rule to use it on very large numbers.

Suggested questions:
- What did you notice?
- How did you work out what to subtract?
- Can you explain your ideas to the class?

Multiplying mayhem (page 25)
☆ *Processes: predict, be systematic, record, look for pattern, explain, co-operate, test ideas*

When the number of steps is shown on a hundred square, the following pattern can be seen. The outer numbers are one-step, the light shaded area two-step, the remaining white section three-step, and the number 77 is the only four-step number.

I	2	3	4	5	6	7	8	9	10
11	12	13	14	15	16	17	18	19	20
21	22	23	24	25	26	27	28	29	30
31	32	33	34	35	36	37	38	39	40
41	42	43	44	45	46	47	48	49	50
51	52	53	54	55	56	57	58	59	60
61	62	63	64	65	66	67	68	69	70
71	72	73	74	75	76	77	78	79	80
81	82	83	84	85	86	87	88	89	90
91	92	93	94	95	96	97	98	99	100

The pattern for a 101–200 square is identical, since most of the multiplications just involve an extra '1 ×' and so give the same single-digit number. (Exceptions are 101, 102, and so on: for example, 102 gives 1 × 0 × 2 = 0.)

Suggested questions:
- What patterns did you notice?
- Were you able to predict how many steps a number had?
- Can you show this on a hundred square?

Wheel patterns (page 26)
☆ *Processes: look for pattern, compare, reason, test ideas, check, visualise*

Discuss with the children how observing patterns can lead to errors being noticed (when one digit does not follow the pattern). Emphasise the importance of using patterns to check their answers. Some children might benefit from the times tables being displayed on the wall for reference. Photocopy extra sheets for the children to continue the investigation. They could look for pairs of tables that make the same wheel pattern. Patterns are as follows:

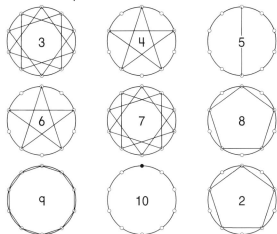

Suggested questions:
- What patterns did you notice?
- Are you sure that every single multiple is correct? What makes you think one might be wrong?

Remainder patterns (page 27)
☆ *Processes: look for pattern, test ideas, predict, reason, record, generalise*

Encourage the children to notice that when a whole number is divided by 5, there will be a remainder unless the number is a multiple of 5.

- If the number is 1 more than a multiple of 5 (numbers ending in 6 or 1), the remainder will be 1.
- If the number is 2 more than a multiple of 5 (numbers ending in 7 or 2), the remainder will be 2.
- If the number is 3 more than a multiple of 5 (numbers ending in 8 or 3), the remainder will be 3.
- If the number is 4 more than a multiple of 5 (numbers ending in 9 or 4), the remainder will be 4.

This pattern continues for all numbers, however large (for example, 13 452 will have a remainder of 2).

The solutions to the extension activity are 10, 19, 28, 37, 46. The children may notice that the sum of the digits is 1 or 10.

Suggested questions:
- What did you notice?
- Can you explain to the class what you found out?

Discuss it (page 28)

☆ *Processes: reason, explain, co-operate, test ideas, record, simplify*

Talk to the class about rules for working in a group: each child should be given the opportunity to have their say; one person could be chosen to make notes; everyone should be able to explain the group's findings to the rest of the class.

Football puzzle This type of puzzle often confuses both adults and children, since it is the same football purchased a second time. If this question involved two separate footballs being bought and then sold at a £1 profit, we can easily see that **Jo makes £2**. Children sometimes *incorrectly* think the following: Jo makes £1 or loses £10, Jo comes out even, Jo loses £30 or makes £40. Each incorrect answer should be discussed, and children encouraged to explain their thinking.

Money puzzle There are five possible solutions:

Tom	Li
£2	£1
£3	£3
£4	£5
£5	£7
£6	£9

Cat puzzle Freya has nine cats now. She had eight cats and her friend had four cats. Now her friend has five cats, which is four less than Freya has.

Coin puzzle Jake and Liam could have any amount from 21p to 29p:

Jake					Liam							
10	5	2	2	2	10	5	2	1	1	1	1	21p each
5	5	5	5	2	10	2	2	2	2	2	2	22p each
10	10	2	2	1	5	5	5	5	1	1	1	23p each
10	10	2	2	2	5	5	5	5	1	1	2	24p each
20	1	1	1	2	5	5	5	5	1	2	2	25p each
20	1	1	2	2	5	5	5	5	2	2	2	26p each
20	2	2	2	1	10	10	2	2	1	1	1	27p each
20	2	2	2	2	10	10	2	2	2	1	1	28p each
20	5	2	1	1	10	10	2	2	2	2	1	29p each

The key to solving the puzzle is to find five coins that make a certain amount and then to find seven coins that make the same amount. The children could be encouraged to find many solutions.

Suggested questions/prompts:
- Tell us about how your group worked together.
- What did your group do well?
- Did you have any problems?

Solving problems

Triple dominoes (page 29)

☆ *Processes: be systematic, check, compare, visualise, look for pattern, record*

There is a maximum of 18 dominoes in the set:

```
000
010   001   020   002
011   101   022   202   012   021   102
112   121   122   212   111   222
```

The solutions can be counted, sorted and checked:

3 blanks	2 blanks	1 blank	no blanks
1 solution	4 solutions	7 solutions	6 solutions
3 ones	2 ones	1 one	no ones
1 solution	4 solutions	7 solutions	6 solutions
3 twos	2 twos	1 two	no twos
1 solution	4 solutions	7 solutions	6 solutions

There are 22 more dominoes if three dots are allowed.

Suggested questions:
- What have you discovered?
- How can you be sure you have found all the dominoes?
- Did you sort them in a particular way?
- How could you check?

Shooting star (page 30)

☆ *Processes: look for pattern, generalise, reason, compare, predict, test ideas*

The children should be encouraged to look for patterns in which sized grids result in which final star. Encourage them to make a list of whether the solutions are grids with odd or even numbers of rows or columns. They are likely to notice first that all square grids result in star C.

The complete rules are given here:

Any square will end in star C.

Any odd × odd rectangle will end in star C.

Any even × odd rectangle will end in star B.
A larger even × smaller even rectangle will end in star B.

Any odd × even rectangle will end in star D.
A smaller even × larger even rectangle will end in star D.

Suggested questions:
- What patterns did you notice in the numbers?
- Have you looked to see whether the numbers are odd or even?

Make way (page 31)

☆ *Processes: make decisions, co-operate, trial and improvement, visualise, reason*

Provide an opportunity for the children to discuss in pairs what they did and any strategies they used.

Suggested questions:
- Who won? Why do you think that player won?
- What strategies did you use?
- Does the player who goes first always win?

Big Wheel challenge: 1 and 2
(pages 32–33)

☆ *Processes: visualise, be systematic, look for pattern, generalise, record, compare, test ideas, check*

Solutions to page 32 are as follows:

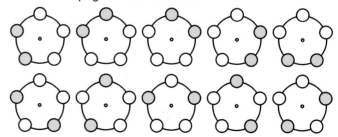

The extension activity has 15 solutions:

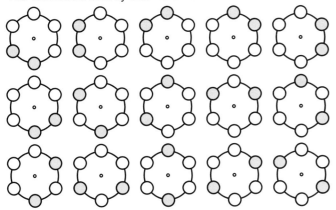

For page 33 there are the following numbers of solutions:

Five cars	If one car has people in:	5 ways
	If three cars have people in:	10 ways
	If four cars have people in:	5 ways
Six cars	If one car has people in:	6 ways
	If three cars have people in:	20 ways
	If four cars have people in:	15 ways

Suggested questions/prompts:

● Explain what you notice to a partner.
● How do you know you have found all the possibilities?

Combination locks (page 34)

☆ *Processes: be systematic, make decisions, test ideas, trial and improvement, visualise, compare, check*

There are 27 combinations of letters (3 × 3 × 3):

LEP	LET	LEN
LIP	LIT	LIN
LOP	LOT	LON
HEP	HET	HEN
HIP	HIT	HIN
HOP	HOT	HON
PEP	PET	PEN
PIP	PIT	PIN
POP	POT	PON

For other wheels with different numbers of letters or wheels, the number of solutions is found by multiplying together the number of letters on each wheel, as many times as there are wheels, for example:

● two wheels with three letters on each would have 3 × 3 = 9 combinations;
● two wheels with four letters on each would have 4 × 4 = 16 combinations;
● four wheels with three letters on each would have 3 × 3 × 3 × 3 = 81 combinations, and so on.

Solutions to the extension activity include:

T	E	D		H	A	M		B	I	T
M	I	N		R	U	T		F	A	N
P	A	T		B	E	G		S	U	D

Suggested questions:

● How many ways did you find?
● How can you be sure that you have found them all?
● Were you systematic?
● In what other ways could you explore these ideas?
● How many real words have you found?

Handling data

New school furniture (page 35)

☆ *Processes: make decisions, co-operate, record, ask own questions, simplify*

Focus the children's attention on teamwork skills as they carry out this activity. Some groups may fail to work well together, but encourage them to explain their problems and to look for ways of overcoming them.

This activity might take place over more than one lesson, perhaps with a planning lesson and then an information collecting lesson.

At the planning stage, ask the groups to record their plan, assigning jobs to members of the group and saying what items they will need in order to collect the information (for example, a chair from each class in the school). At various points in the lesson, stop the groups and ask for feedback on their progress, encouraging the children to comment on any good teamwork within their group. Once the children have gathered information (including measuring the appropriate dimensions of chairs and tables for different age groups) and have written an order list, more confident children could use catalogues to work out the cost of the purchase, using a calculator if necessary.

Suggested questions:

● What did you decide?
● How well did you get on as a group?
● What have you learned about working in a group?
● How could you improve the way you work together?

Pet prizes (page 36)

☆ *Processes: simplify, record, predict, generalise, test ideas, make decisions, be systematic*

Discuss the ways in which the children choose to record their results. A table of results might look like this:

	M	Tu	W	Th	F	Sa	Su	Total
hamster	1	1	1	1	1	1	1	7
cat		2	2	2	2	2	2	12
rabbit			3	3	3	3	3	15
dog				4	4	4	4	16
rat					5	5	5	15
goat						6	6	12
horse							7	7
Total no. of pets =								84

Lucy will have more dogs than any other type of pet. Encourage the children to note the symmetrical nature of the numbers in the table and to suggest reasons for this.

For the extension activity, the numbers of pets will follow this pattern: 10, 18, 24, 28, 30, 30, 28, 24, 18, 10. So, Lucy will have more rats and goats than any other type of pet.

Suggested questions:

● Explain to your partner what you notice.
● Why do you think this could be?
● How could you show what you have found on a poster?
● Which pets are there fewest of?
● How many more rabbits are there than hamsters?

Measures, shape and space

Extra square: 1 and 2 (pages 37–38)

☆ *Processes: visualise, trial and improvement, record, look for pattern, simplify, test ideas, be systematic, compare, check*

The children may begin to notice that, once one square has been marked with a cross, all the pieces can be rotated in the same arrangement to cross off three more squares. They will find that all the squares in the grid can be crossed. By recording their findings, the children can focus on being systematic. Emphasise that recording is vital for showing others what you did, comparing solutions, and as a personal reference that can be looked back on.

Here are the nine solutions to the extension activity. Rotations and reflections are classed as the same.

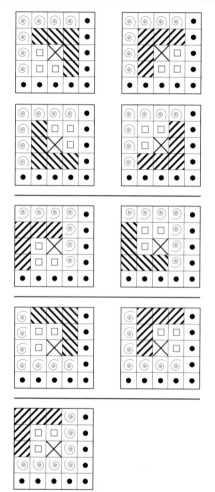

Suggested questions:

- How could you group your solutions?
- Are all these exactly the same, but rotated?
- What is different about these two solutions?

It's all in the shape (page 39)

☆ *Processes: explain, co-operate, compare, visualise, record*

This activity focuses attention on describing accurately what the shapes on each card look like, and where the triangle and rectangle lie in relation to each other. Encourage the children to use specific language, such as the words in the box on the sheet. In the extension activity,

they will need to make sure that their descriptions do not apply to more than one card.

Suggested questions:

- How could you describe these shapes?
- Which word could you use to describe where the triangle is?
- What about the rectangle?
- In what way is this card different from this one?
- Does your description only fit this card, or could it describe one of the other cards too?

Clock angles (page 40)

☆ *Processes: be systematic, co-operate, visualise, record, compare*

There are 22 different positions of the hands, which gives a total of 44 solutions in one day (half of which are am times and half pm times). The approximate times are:

12:16	12:49	6:16	6:49
1:22	1:55	7:22	7:55
2:27		8:27	
3:00	3:33	9:00	9:33
4:05	4:38	10:05	10:38
5:11	5:44	11:11	11:44

The children should be encouraged to notice and describe patterns in the times (for example, 8:27 and 2:27; 12:16 and 6:16). As a further extension, the approximate number of minutes between consecutive times (about 33 minutes) can be explored.

Suggested questions:

- What patterns have you noticed?
- Between which hours is there only one right angle?
- How can you be sure you have found all the times?

Point patterns (page 41)

☆ *Processes: look for pattern, explain, reason, test ideas, check*

The children should notice the following patterns:

- For the bottom-left corner, the co-ordinates go (1, 1) (2, 2) (3, 3) (4, 4).
  The first and second co-ordinates are the same.
- For the top-left corner, the co-ordinates go (1, 10) (2, 9) (3, 8) (4, 7).
  The sum of the first and second co-ordinates is 11.
- For the bottom-right corner, the co-ordinates go (8, 1) (7, 2) (6, 3) (5, 4).
  The sum of the first and second co-ordinates is 9.
- For the top-right corner, the co-ordinates go (8, 10) (7, 9) (6, 8) (5, 7).
  The first and second co-ordinates each decrease by 1.

Suggested questions:

- What do you notice?
- Can you explain to the class what you found out?

Star gazing (page 42)

☆ *Processes: visualise, generalise, test ideas, reason, predict, look for pattern, estimate*

The children should notice that the square and triangle do not produce stars, and that the irregular pentagon does not produce points at every side (as it has two adjacent right angles and so the extended lines are parallel). The other regular shapes all produce complete stars.

Whilst you may not wish to discuss the following fully with the children, it is given for your information.

The main feature that determines whether two sides join to make a point is whether the two angles at those corners have a total greater than 180°.

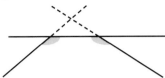

Thus all regular pentagons, hexagons, heptagons, octagons, and so on will make stars, since all their angles are greater than 90°; so will any of the aforementioned shapes that are irregular but have adjacent angles greater than 180°, for example:

Triangles cannot have angles greater than 180°, so can never produce the point of a star in this way.

The angles of squares and rectangles are right angles, so these shapes do not work. In other quadrilaterals, it is impossible for all adjacent angles to have a total greater than 180°, so whilst they can make some star points, they will not make a complete star.

The children will obviously not be describing their thinking in these terms, but should be able to discuss which shapes have obtuse and acute angles. They should notice that adjacent right angles produce parallel lines that never meet, and that regular shapes with five or more sides seem to work.

Suggested questions/prompts:
● What patterns do you notice?
● Explain your thinking to a partner.

Ribbon predictions (page 43)

☆ *Processes: predict, visualise, test ideas, compare*
Once the activity has been completed, the nets could be put on a wall as a stimulating display to promote discussion and encourage predictions.

Suggested questions:
● Which of your predictions were correct?
● Can you make some nets of your own?

Starman (page 44)

☆ *Processes: record, visualise, make decisions, compare*
Before starting, clarify with the children whether they will talk about the robot's left/right, or left/right as the children see it. Once the instructions have been completed, ask the children to compare approaches and to say which ways they prefer and why. They could be asked to repeat the activity using a more effective approach.

Suggested questions:
● Whose instructions did you find easier to understand?
● Why do you think that was?

Tile tricks: 1 and 2 (pages 45–46)

☆ *Processes: visualise, look for pattern, make decisions, predict, co-operate, test ideas, record*
The children could explore which sets of numbers produce symmetrical patterns or reflections of each other.

Solutions:

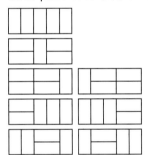

Suggested questions:
● What patterns have you made?
● What is special about the numbers?
● Is your pattern symmetrical?
● What other questions could you ask?

Exercise mats (page 47)

☆ *Processes: be systematic, visualise, check, compare, record, look for pattern*
There are eight distinct arrangements, six of which make three pairs of rotated or reflected patterns:

Suggested questions:
● If the hall was turned through a half turn, which arrangements would look the same?
● Are any of your patterns the same but upside down?
● How do you know you have found all the arrangements?

Spiralling out of control (page 48)

☆ *Processes: estimate, co-operate, predict, reason, test ideas, check*
Estimating is a valuable using and applying skill and this activity encourages the children to estimate lengths to the nearest half centimetre.

Suggested questions/prompts:
● How good were your estimates?
● Did you get better each time you estimated?
● How far away was your estimate?

Take the challenge

Use trial and improvement and be systematic

☆ Look at the key. Use it to make numbers that spell out real three- or four-letter words.

Example: two thousand   M
           three hundred   E
           seventy   N
           one   D

Use only one letter from each section.

☆ Record your numbers and words like this:
2371 = MEND
6308 = WET

Key

B	eight thousand
W	six thousand
L	four thousand
M	two thousand
A	nine hundred
E	three hundred
N	seventy
S	fifty
T	eight
D	one

• **Try these challenges. Work on scrap paper.**

Challenge 1
What is the largest **even** number you can make in this way?

Challenge 2
Which word has a number closest to 5000?

Challenge 3
How many words can you make with numbers between 800 and 3000?

• **Make a poster to display your answers to these challenges.**

Now try this!

• **Now follow this challenge.**

Challenge 4
Write words which have one letter different, like BEN**D** and BEN**T**.
Find the difference between the numbers.
What is the largest difference you can find?

Teachers' note This activity provides an opportunity for children to practise reading and writing numbers in words and figures in an open way. They could work in pairs to encourage co-operation skills and discussion. At the start of the lesson, demonstrate the activity and point out that when a digit in a number is zero, it means that there are none in that column and no letter is used. So a four-digit number can make a three- or even two-letter word (for example, 6308 = WET, 2300 = ME).

Developing Numeracy
Using & Applying Maths
Year 4
© A & C BLACK

Money matters

In her purse, Mrs Mayer has one banknote and three coins of the same value.

How much money could I have in my purse?

- | Predict | how many answers there might be to her question. _____

- Test your prediction by writing all the possible amounts. Try to be systematic.

£5.03
£5.06

- Set out your solutions in a table, like this.
- Explain to a partner how this helps you.

Coins	Notes		
	£5	£10	£20
1p	£5.03		
2p	£5.06		

Teachers' note First revise £.p notation and discuss the different coins and notes used in Britain. The extension activity helps the children to develop a systematic approach so that the full set of solutions can be found.

Developing Numeracy
Using & Applying Maths
Year 4
© A & C BLACK

Printing patterns

This printing wheel has six shapes on it. When you roll the wheel, the shapes are printed in a line. The pattern of shapes keeps on repeating.

triangle	square	pentagon	hexagon	heptagon	octagon	...
1st	2nd	3rd	4th	5th	6th	

- **Write the first ┃ten┃ position numbers for each shape.**

triangle   1st, 7th, _____

square   _____

pentagon   _____

hexagon   _____

heptagon   _____

octagon   _____

- **Talk to a partner about the position numbers for each shape.**

Are they odd or even?

What about shapes that have an even number of sides?

Now try this!

- **Explain how you can be certain of these things:**

The shape in the 80th position has an even number of sides.

The shape in the 120th position will be an octagon.

If a shape's position number is an **odd multiple of 3**, it will be a pentagon.

- **Discuss two other things that you are certain of.**

Teachers' note Encourage the children to discuss the patterns in pairs and to suggest reasons for them. They should consider which shapes have odd position numbers and which have even ones, and think about whether the shapes have an odd or even number of sides.

**Developing Numeracy
Using & Applying Maths
Year 4
© A & C BLACK**

Be systematic and reason

Gita is thinking of a number.

My number has three digits.
The sum of the digits is 6.

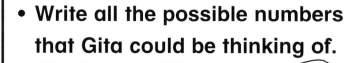

Example: 312 → 3 + 1 + 2

- **Write all the possible numbers that Gita could be thinking of.**

Use zeros if you need to. 105

105

- **How many of the numbers lie in each of these groups?**

Numbers: from 100 to 400   from 401 to 700   above 700

- **Write the numbers in order, from smallest to largest.**

- **What if the sum of the digits was** 12 **? Investigate in which group most of the possible numbers would lie.**

Teachers' note Encourage the children to work systematically, finding all the possible permutations of each set of digits (for example, 312, 321, 231…). Ask them to suggest the largest digit that can be used in a number. When they have observed where the majority of the possible numbers lie, they should suggest reasons for this. The extension activity can be developed into an extensive investigation to find which sums of digits result in the majority of numbers falling in a particular group.

Developing Numeracy
Using & Applying Maths
Year 4
© A & C BLACK

17

Hair wash calendar

On New Year's Eve, six friends wash their hair.

Kim washes her hair **every six days**.
She washes it on January 6th, 12th…
Tom washes his hair **every five days**.
He washes it on January 5th, 10th…
Zoe washes her hair **every four days**.
Ali washes his hair **every three days**,
Lucy every two days and
Sam every day.

On which dates do you <u>think</u> the most hair washes will take place?

- **On this calendar, record the dates on which each child washes his or her hair.**

January

1st	2nd	3rd	4th	5th	6th	7th
8th	9th	10th	11th	12th	13th	14th
15th	16th	17th	18th	19th	20th	21st
22nd	23rd	24th	25th	26th	27th	28th
29th	30th	31st				

- **On which dates do the most hair washes take place?**

_____

- **Use different-coloured pencils to colour dates on which the same number of hair washes take place.**

Teachers' note Discuss ways of recording, such as using the first letter of each child's name. Talk about why some strategies might not be as useful: for example, if tallying is used, mistakes cannot be checked. Ask the children to discuss any patterns they notice in the arrangements (see page 7). As an extension, ask the children to work out the next date when all six children will wash their hair (see page 7 for solution).

**Developing Numeracy
Using & Applying Maths
Year 4
© A & C BLACK**

Tea-time for Toby

There are many ways in which
Toby can climb these five steps:

Tea-time,
Toby!

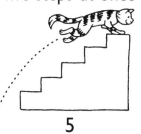

one step at a time
two steps, then three steps
five steps at once

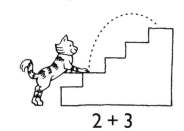

| + | + | + | + |
2 + 3
5

- **Find all the different ways in which Toby can climb:**

climb:	Different ways	Number of ways
one step		
two steps		
three steps		
four steps		
five steps	| + | + | + | + | 2 + 3 5	
six steps		

- **Predict the number of ways for:**

  seven steps _____   **eight** steps _____

- **Explain your thinking to a partner.**

Teachers' note The children should check their solutions by ensuring that each addition totals the number of steps. Encourage them to work systematically to find all the solutions. When all the solutions have been found, the children should be able to see patterns in the numbers, which will enable them to predict the number of ways for seven and eight steps (see page 8). As an extension, ask the children to predict the number of ways for nine, ten and eleven steps.

**Developing Numeracy
Using & Applying Maths
Year 4**
© A & C BLACK

19

Split decisions

The digits $\boxed{5}\boxed{6}\boxed{1}\boxed{3}$ can be split in different ways. When the numbers are added, they give the same answer.

$\boxed{5}\boxed{6}+\boxed{1}\boxed{3}=69$ ✔

$\boxed{5}+\boxed{6}\boxed{1}+\boxed{3}=69$

Not all digits work this way.

$\boxed{3}\boxed{2}+\boxed{4}\boxed{1}=73$ ✘

$\boxed{3}+\boxed{2}\boxed{4}+\boxed{1}=28$

- **Test these digits to see whether they work.**

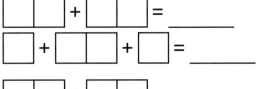

What is special about the digits that work?

$\boxed{2}\boxed{7}+\boxed{4}\boxed{9}=$ _____

$\boxed{2}+\boxed{7}\boxed{4}+\boxed{9}=$ _____

$\boxed{1}\boxed{2}+\boxed{1}\boxed{4}=$ _____

$\boxed{1}+\boxed{2}\boxed{1}+\boxed{4}=$ _____

$\boxed{1}\boxed{5}+\boxed{4}\boxed{2}=$ _____

$\boxed{1}+\boxed{5}\boxed{4}+\boxed{2}=$ _____

$\boxed{3}\boxed{7}+\boxed{4}\boxed{1}=$ _____

$\boxed{3}+\boxed{7}\boxed{4}+\boxed{1}=$ _____

- **Now try some digits of your own.**

$\boxed{\ }\boxed{\ }+\boxed{\ }\boxed{\ }=$ _____

$\boxed{\ }+\boxed{\ }\boxed{\ }+\boxed{\ }=$ _____

$\boxed{\ }\boxed{\ }+\boxed{\ }\boxed{\ }=$ _____

$\boxed{\ }+\boxed{\ }\boxed{\ }+\boxed{\ }=$ _____

$\boxed{\ }\boxed{\ }+\boxed{\ }\boxed{\ }=$ _____

$\boxed{\ }+\boxed{\ }\boxed{\ }+\boxed{\ }=$ _____

$\boxed{\ }\boxed{\ }+\boxed{\ }\boxed{\ }=$ _____

$\boxed{\ }+\boxed{\ }\boxed{\ }+\boxed{\ }=$ _____

$\boxed{\ }\boxed{\ }+\boxed{\ }\boxed{\ }=$ _____

$\boxed{\ }+\boxed{\ }\boxed{\ }+\boxed{\ }=$ _____

$\boxed{\ }\boxed{\ }+\boxed{\ }\boxed{\ }=$ _____

$\boxed{\ }+\boxed{\ }\boxed{\ }+\boxed{\ }=$ _____

Now try this!

- **Look at the first and third digits in sets that work. Now look at the second digit.**
- **Can the fourth digit be any digit?**

What do you notice?

Teachers' note Encourage the children to find other sets of digits that, when split in these ways, give the same answer (they could use squared paper for recording). The sets of digits that work could be compiled as a class list on the board to help the children find patterns. Once the children have found patterns in the digits that work, they could create a poster or chart explaining what they have found.

**Developing Numeracy
Using & Applying Maths
Year 4
© A & C BLACK**

Pattern codes

Anna has shaded a **symmetrical** pattern on this grid. Look at how she works out its pattern code.

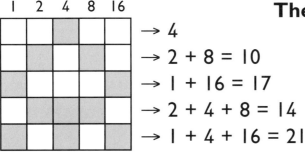

$\rightarrow$ 4
$\rightarrow$ 2 + 8 = 10
$\rightarrow$ 1 + 16 = 17
$\rightarrow$ 2 + 4 + 8 = 14
$\rightarrow$ 1 + 4 + 16 = 21

The code is  4, 10, 17, 14, 21

- ## Shade symmetrical patterns. Write their pattern codes.

| 1 | 2 | 4 | 8 | 16 |

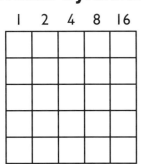

| 1 | 2 | 4 | 8 | 16 |

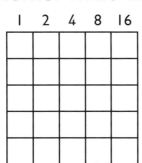

| 1 | 2 | 4 | 8 | 16 |

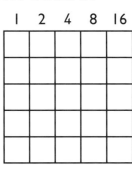

- ## Try these grids.

Remember to make the patterns symmetrical.

| 1 | 2 | 4 | 8 | 16 | 32 |

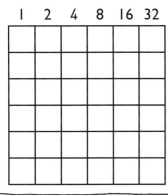

| 1 | 2 | 4 | 8 | 16 | 32 |

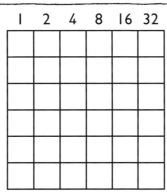

| 1 | 2 | 4 | 8 | 16 | 32 |

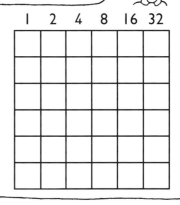

- ## On squared paper, shade some patterns with │ two lines of symmetry │.
- ## Write their pattern codes.

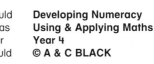

Teachers' note Check that the children shade symmetrical patterns. Discuss that the patterns could have horizontal, vertical or diagonal lines of symmetry. The children might notice that if a pattern has a horizontal mirror line, then the code will be palindromic, i.e. it will be the same when reversed (for example, 12, 18, 45, 45, 18, 12). Provide squared paper for the extension activity. The children could copy out their codes for a partner to draw the patterns.

**Developing Numeracy
Using & Applying Maths
Year 4
© A & C BLACK**

Bedroom makeover

Make decisions and visualise

You have won a £2000 bedroom 'makeover'.

- **Choose what you want from the lists below, but do not spend more than £2000. Your bedroom should have these things:**

  a bed, a wardrobe, paint on the walls, a carpet, a duvet cover, a pair of curtains, a chair and desk, and any electrical things you can afford!

- **Record your choices and the total price on a separate piece of paper.**

Bed
Raised bed (comes with desk and chair underneath)	£600
Bunk beds	£300
Double bed	£200
Single bed	£100
Your own design	£500

Wardrobe
One so big you can hide in it!	£400
Double wardrobe	£300
One with a big mirror	£200
Single wardrobe	£100
Your own design	£500

Paint colours
Pink	£30
Blue	£20
Cream	£15
White	£10
All other colours	£50

Carpet patterns
Flowers	£400
Stars	£300
Spots	£200
Plain	£100
Your own design	£500

Duvet designs
Pictures on it	£80
Football design	£70
Stripes	£60
Plain	£30
Your own design	£100

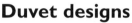

Curtains
Pink	£70
Blue	£50
Cream	£40
White	£30
All other colours	£80

Chairs and desks
Computer desk	£200
Swivel chair	£100
Armchair	£80
Chair and desk set	£150
Your own design	£300

Electrical things
Computer	£600
Widescreen TV	£400
Stereo	£200
Portable TV	£150
DVD player	£100

Teachers' note This activity encourages the children to make decisions and choices based on particular criteria. They will need to work out whether they can afford all their first choices; it is likely that they will have to make compromises and alter some choices in favour of others as they go along. As an extension, the children could write descriptions of the cheapest and most expensive bedrooms (within the budget), discussing the advantages and disadvantages of each.

Developing Numeracy
Using & Applying Maths
Year 4
© A & C BLACK

Earring designs

Josh and Ella are making earrings from small pieces of wire.
Ella joins the wires with a small bead. Josh fixes on the hook.

wire pieces	10p each
beads	15p each
hooks	25p each

- How much does it cost to make each of these earrings?

Use this price list.

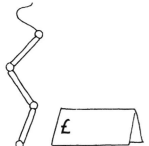
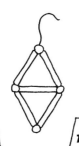
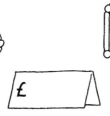
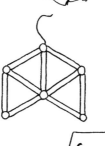
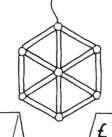

£   £   £   £

- Design earrings that cost each of these amounts.

£1.00   £1.85   £2.80   £3.65

- Is it possible to make an earring that costs 80p ?

Teachers' note Point out that each earring must have a hook which is attached to a bead. This activity encourages the children to begin reasoning about how particular totals are possible: for example, if the total cost is even, there must be an odd number of beads, since there can be only one 25p hook. If the total ends in 5, there must be an even number of beads. Encourage the children to compare their solutions.

Developing Numeracy Using & Applying Maths Year 4 © A & C BLACK

Reason and look for patterns

This machine is magic because the output number is the same as the input number.

input **output**

$6 \rightarrow \times 3 \rightarrow -12 \rightarrow 6$

- **Make up your own magic machines.**

Think carefully about what you could multiply by and then subtract to get back to your input number.

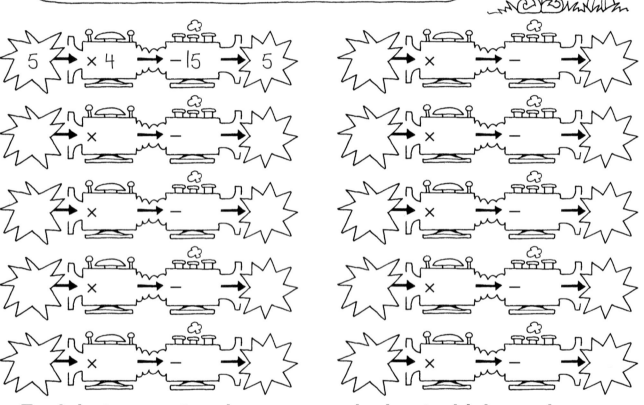

$5 \rightarrow \times 4 \rightarrow -15 \rightarrow 5$

- **Explain to a partner how you worked out which number to subtract.**

Now try this!

- **Make up some magic machines using these operations:** [+] and [÷]

Think carefully about what to add, so that you will be able to divide.

Teachers' note Demonstrate the idea of a magic machine and ensure the children realise that they need to work out what to multiply by and then subtract to get back to the start number. For the extension activity, the children will need to think about what numbers to add and then divide by to get back to the start number.

**Developing Numeracy
Using & Applying Maths
Year 4
© A & C BLACK**

Multiplying mayhem

Make predictions and be systematic

☆ Write a two-digit number.   27

☆ Multiply its digits together. $2 \times 7 = 14$

☆ If the answer is a single-digit number,
STOP. If not, multiply its digits together. $1 \times 4 = 4$

☆ Keep going until you get a single-digit number.

We say 27 is a two-step number, as it takes two multiplications to reach a single-digit number.

• **Investigate which two-digit number has the most steps.**

• **Talk to a partner about three things that you noticed when you were trying out numbers.**

You need a hundred square.

• **Find where all the one-step numbers are.**

• **What about the other step numbers?**

Teachers' note Some children may need to refer to tables facts. Encourage the children to co-operate with others when investigating all the two-digit numbers. For the extension activity, the children will find it helpful to colour a hundred square using a key (such as one-step = red, two-step = yellow…). Ask them to describe patterns they notice when investigating numbers in this way. The activity could be extended to include numbers up to 300 (for example, 123 → 1 × 2 × 3 = 6).

**Developing Numeracy
Using & Applying Maths
Year 4
© A & C BLACK**

Wheel patterns

Look for patterns and make comparisons

☆ Choose a times table, such as the **3** times table.

☆ On scrap paper, write the multiples in order.
Ring the units digit of each multiple.

Example: ③, ⑥, ⑨, 1②, 1⑤ ...

☆ Join these digits in order on a wheel. Use a ruler.

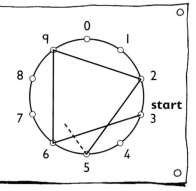

• **Investigate what pattern each times table makes.**

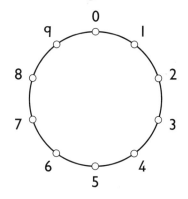
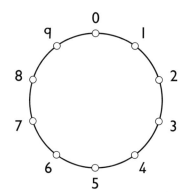
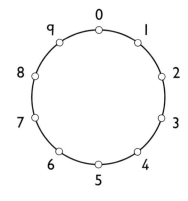

3 times table

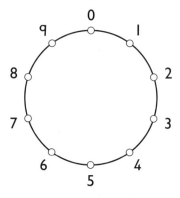
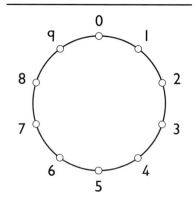
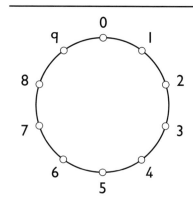

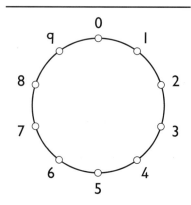
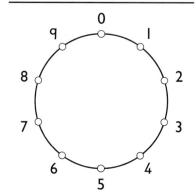
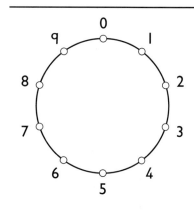

Teachers' note Revise the term 'multiple' and ensure the children understand that they should be focusing on the units/ones digits of the multiples, and joining them in order on the wheels. Ask them to predict what will happen with tables such as 5 and 10. As an extension, the children could investigate other multiples (for example, by counting in steps of 11, 13 or 25). Ask them to suggest reasons why different tables produce certain results.

Developing Numeracy
Using & Applying Maths
Year 4
© A & C BLACK

Remainder patterns

Look for patterns, test your ideas and make predictions

- **Divide** each number **by 5** and write the remainder.

- **Colour the start numbers using this key:**

Colour	Remainder
yellow	1
red	2
green	3
blue	4

41 ÷ 5 = 8 r 1

26 _____

38 _____ 21 _____ 33 _____

29 _____ 16 _____ 12 _____

17 _____ 34 _____ 48 _____

19 _____ 52 _____ 37 _____

- **On this chart, list the numbers that have each remainder. Then test other numbers to 100.**

remainder 1	remainder 2	remainder 3	remainder 4
41,			

- **Write about any patterns you notice.**

_____

_____

_____

_____

- **Investigate** dividing by 9 . **Find all the numbers up to 50 that have a remainder of 1. What patterns do you notice?**

- **Investigate other remainders when you divide by 9.**

Teachers' note Ensure that the children understand the idea of a remainder when a number is divided. Some children may benefit from having a list of the multiples of 5 to 50 or 100 on display. Encourage the children to talk to each other about the patterns they notice and to test other numbers before writing about the patterns. They could then use the patterns to predict the remainders when other numbers are divided by 5.

Developing Numeracy
Using & Applying Maths
Year 4
© A & C BLACK

Discuss it

Reason, explain and co-operate

Football puzzle

Jo buys a football for £8.
She sells it for £9.
Then she buys the same
football back again for £10.
Finally, she sells it for £11.

- **How much money does
Jo make or lose?**

Money puzzle

At the start, Tom and Li
each have a whole number
of pounds less than £10.
If Tom gives Li one of his
pounds, Li will have twice
as much money as Tom.

- **How much money could
each boy have at the start?**

Cat puzzle

Freya has lots of cats.
Her friend has half as
many cats as Freya.
Freya and her friend
each get one new cat.
Now Freya has four more
cats than her friend has.

- **How many cats does
Freya have now?**

Coin puzzle

Jake has five coins.
Liam has seven coins.
They both have the same
amount of money which is
between 20p and 30p.

- **How much money could
they both have?**

Teachers' note Begin the lesson by talking to the class about rules for working in a group (see page 10). Split the class into groups of three or four, and tell them that they are going to discuss a puzzle and write a group answer to it. Cut out the cards and give one to each group, or let the groups tackle a puzzle of their choice. See page 10 for solutions.

**Developing Numeracy
Using & Applying Maths
Year 4
© A & C BLACK**

Triple dominoes

A special set of dominoes is being made.
Each domino has three sections.
In each section there could be one dot,
two dots or no dots.

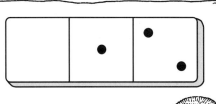

- **Draw the dots to show all the dominoes that could be in the set.**

You may not need to use all these outlines.

- **How many more dominoes could there be if three dots were allowed?**

Teachers' note Ensure the children understand that no two dominoes in the set should be the same, and that a 0, 1, 2 domino is the same as a 2, 1, 0 domino, just rotated. Discuss ways of recording solutions to the extension activity (for example, 013, 023, 033…). Some children might prefer to have a second blank sheet or squared paper for recording the solutions.

**Developing Numeracy
Using & Applying Maths
Year 4
© A & C BLACK**

Shooting star

Look for patterns and generalise

Star **A** shoots out a laser beam. If the beam hits the sides of the grid, it bounces off at **right angles** until it hits star **B**, **C** or **D**.

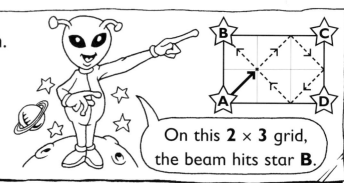

On this **2 × 3** grid, the beam hits star **B**.

• **In each grid, which star will the laser beam hit?**

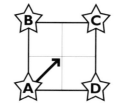

2 × 5 grid
Beam hits star ☐

2 × 2 grid
Beam hits star ☐

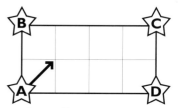

2 × 4 grid
Beam hits star ☐

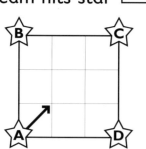

3 × 3 grid
Beam hits star ☐

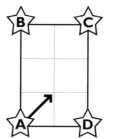

3 × 2 grid
Beam hits star ☐

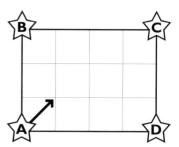

3 × 4 grid
Beam hits star ☐

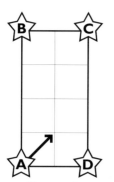

4 × 2 grid
Beam hits star ☐

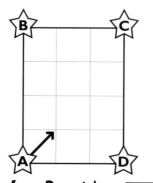

4 × 3 grid
Beam hits star ☐

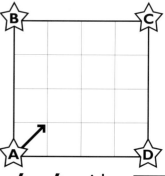

4 × 4 grid
Beam hits star ☐

Now try this!

• **List the grids that end at star B, C and D.**
• **Predict what will happen with other grids. Test this on squared paper.**

	B	C	D
2 × 3			

Teachers' note Ensure that the children understand the path followed by the laser beam, and make sure they use rulers. You may need to demonstrate drawing the path of the beam several times on the board. Provide the children with squared paper to test other grids, and encourage them to predict the nature of the grid that would end at each of the stars, paying attention to odd and even numbers, and which of the two numbers is larger. See page 10 for more information.

**Developing Numeracy
Using & Applying Maths
Year 4
© A & C BLACK**

Make way

Make decisions

- **Play this game with a partner.** (**You need** four counters each.)

☆ Place your counters on the circles.

☆ Take turns to move your counters forwards, backwards or sideways, but **not** diagonally.

☆ You can jump over a counter (including your own), if there is a space on the other side.

☆ The winner is the first player to get all their counters to the other side.

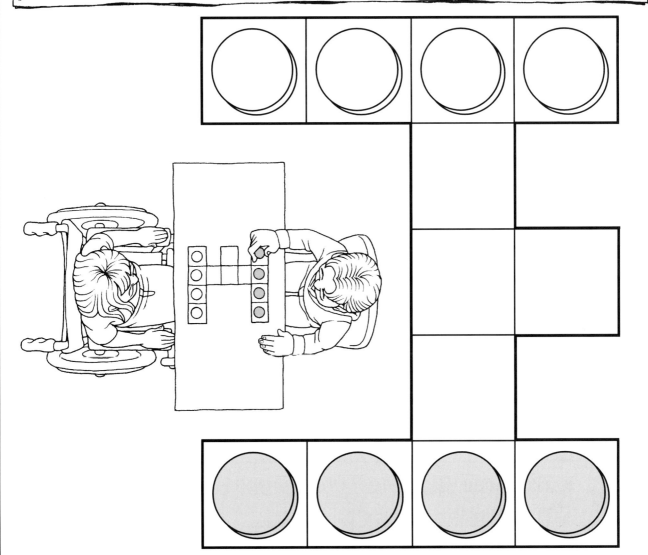

- **With your partner, write a list of things that you noticed. Did the player who went first always win?**

Teachers' note Each pair will need four counters in one colour and four in another, and one copy of this sheet. Ensure that the children understand the rules of the game, and demonstrate the moves with the whole class at the start of the lesson. Encourage the children to see that blocking their opponent creates a stalemate situation and, in order to get their counters to the other side, they have to create space.

Developing Numeracy
Using & Applying Maths
Year 4
© A & C BLACK

Big Wheel challenge: 1

This Big Wheel has **five** cars.
Two cars have people in and three
cars are empty.
The cars with people in are shaded.
The wheel turns clockwise.

• **Shade the cars to show all the different ways this could look.**

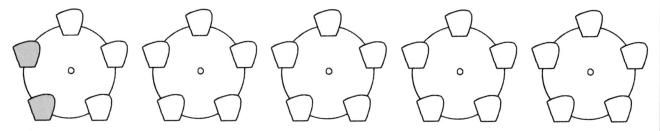

This time, two different cars have people
in. The other three cars are empty.

• **Shade the cars to show all the different ways this could look.**

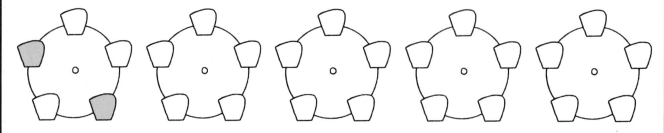

• **You need** *Big Wheel challenge: 2.*
• **This Big Wheel has** six **cars.
Two of the cars have people in.
Shade the cars to show all the
different ways this could look.**

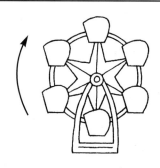

Teachers' note You could demonstrate this at the start of the lesson using counters in two colours stuck onto a card circle, as in the first picture. Rotate the circle to show how the arrangement of counters looks as the wheel turns. The children will need the bottom half of page 33 when tackling the extension activity. Discuss systematic approaches that allow them to be sure that they have found all the solutions.

**Developing Numeracy
Using & Applying Maths
Year 4
© A & C BLACK**

Big Wheel challenge: 2

Look for patterns and generalise

• **Investigate other ways a Big Wheel could look when** [one] **car,** [three] **cars or** [four] **cars have people in.**

Look for patterns in the numbers of ways you find.

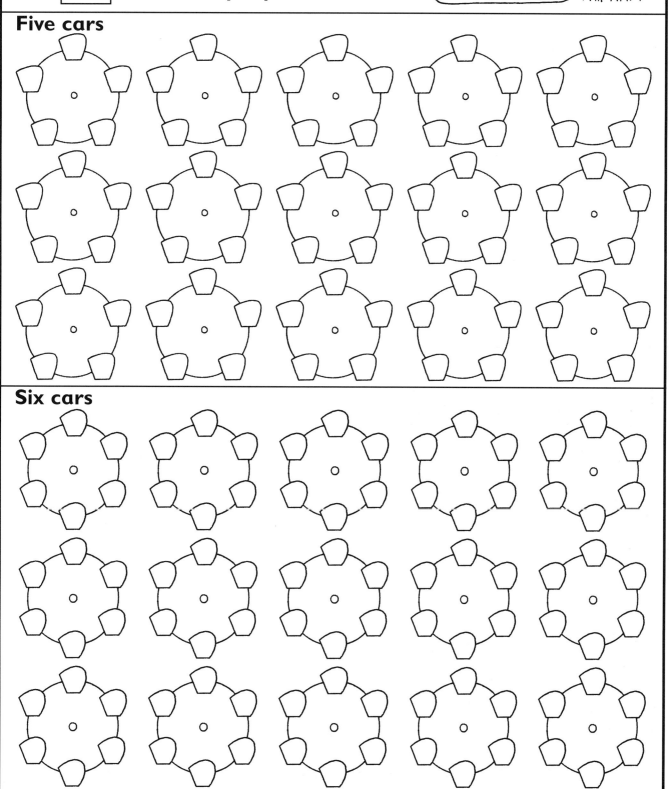

Five cars

Six cars

Teachers' note Use this sheet with the extension activity on page 32. It can also be used as a follow-on activity from page 32, for which each child may need up to three copies of the sheet. Encourage the children to pursue their own lines of enquiry: for example, some children could work in pairs or groups to compile a set of all the ways that a wheel with six cars could look when two cars are full. Another group or pair could explore the ways it could look with three full cars, and so on.

**Developing Numeracy
Using & Applying Maths
Year 4
© A & C BLACK**

Combination locks

On this suitcase, the combination lock has three letters on each wheel. Here are some combinations that the lock can show. Some are real words and others are not.

HIT   HEP   LON
POT   PIP   HEN

L E P
H   I   T
P O N

- **List all the possible combinations.**
- **Tick the real words.**

You may need a dictionary to help you.

I found ☐ combinations.

- **On a separate piece of paper, list all the possible combinations for this lock.**
- **Tick the real words.**

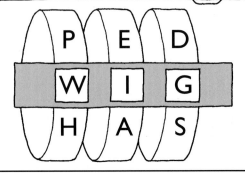

P E D
W   I   G
H A S

- **Find nine other letters for the lock which will give at least 20 real words.**

There must be three letters on each wheel.

Teachers' note Suggest that for this activity, names can be included as real words. Provide dictionaries and encourage discussion about which combinations are real words. As a follow-up, the children could explore the number of combinations for a lock that has three wheels, with one, two, four or five letters on each wheel. They could also explore the number of combinations where there are more or fewer wheels on the lock: for example, four wheels with three letters on each wheel.

Developing Numeracy
Using & Applying Maths
Year 4
© A & C BLACK

New school furniture

Make decisions and co-operate

Your headteacher wants to replace all the chairs and tables in the school.

- **Work in a group to help collect information.**
  Think about these things:

What information do you need to know?

Are all the chairs and tables in the school the same size?

What sizes are they?　　　　Who uses them?

What shapes are the tables?
Are they circles, hexagons, rectangles…?

About how many of each size and shape will you need?

How will you collect this information and how will you record it?

Who will measure tables and who will measure chairs? What measuring equipment will you need?

How will you decide how many chairs and tables you need? Who could you ask? Will you have to count them all?

- **Once you have collected all the information you need, write an order list for the replacement chairs and tables.**

Teachers' note This activity is intended to be an information gathering exercise where the children, in groups, make decisions about what information to collect and how to collect it. Explain to the children that the headteacher wants to replace the old furniture with *identical* new furniture.

Developing Numeracy
Using & Applying Maths
Year 4
© A & C BLACK

Pet prizes

Lucky Lucy has won a competition.

Each day, for one week, she is sent prizes.

But… the prizes are all pets!

On Monday she is sent: **1 hamster**.

On Tuesday she is sent: **1 hamster**, **2 cats**.

On Wednesday she is sent: **1 hamster**, **2 cats**, **3 rabbits**.

The pattern continues like this. The next pets she is sent are dogs, then rats, then goats, then horses.

Which animal will I have most of at the end of the week?

- **To answer Lucy's question, think about how many days there are and how many of each type of pet.**

- **Choose how you are going to record your results.**

- **How many pets is Lucy sent in total?** _____

 • **If Lucy won prizes for ten days, which pet would she have most of after ten days?** _____

Teachers' note This activity requires the children to simplify the problem, by taking each day or animal at a time, and to make decisions about how to record the information: for example, in a table. Patterns in the table could be explored, and this could lead to further predictions about the numbers of animals sent if the sending of prizes went on for more than seven or ten days. For the extension activity, suggest that the children make up new pets that Lucy could be sent on days eight to ten.

**Developing Numeracy
Using & Applying Maths
Year 4**
© A & C BLACK

Extra square: 1

Visualise, use trial and improvement, and record information

• **Follow these instructions.**

☆ Cut out the shapes below.

☆ Arrange them on this grid so that only one small square is uncovered.

☆ Mark the uncovered square with a cross.

☆ Try different ways. Find out which squares can be marked with a cross.

• **Explain to a partner what you have found out.**

• **How many different ways can you arrange the shapes so that the central square is uncovered?**

• **Record your solutions on Extra square: 2.**

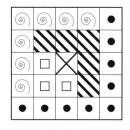

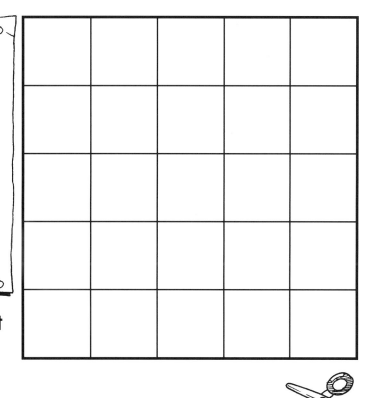

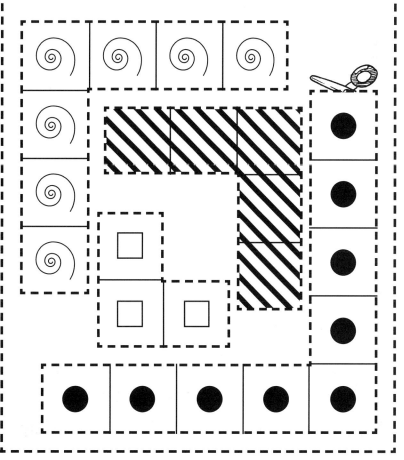

Teachers' note For the extension activity, each child will need a copy of page 38. Encourage the children to compare their solutions with others and to begin to compile a group or class set. The completed grids could be cut out and sorted into groups: for example, those solutions which have the two largest pieces around the edge of the grid; those with the second largest piece lying inside the largest piece; and those that are rotations or reflections of other solutions.

Developing Numeracy
Using & Applying Maths
Year 4
© A & C BLACK

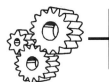

Extra square: 2

Visualise, use trial and improvement, and record information

**Developing Numeracy
Using & Applying Maths
Year 4**
© A & C BLACK

It's all in the shape

Each card shows a rectangle and a triangle.

The shapes often touch or overlap.

- **Try this activity with a partner.**

☆ Cut out the cards. Spread them out face down.

☆ Pick a card. Describe the shapes for your partner to draw them on a piece of paper.

☆ Compare the drawing with your card. Is it accurate?

☆ Take turns to describe and draw.

Use words like these.

| equilateral | isosceles | right angle | length | width | edge | vertex |
| horizontal | vertical | diagonal | in the middle | inside | below |

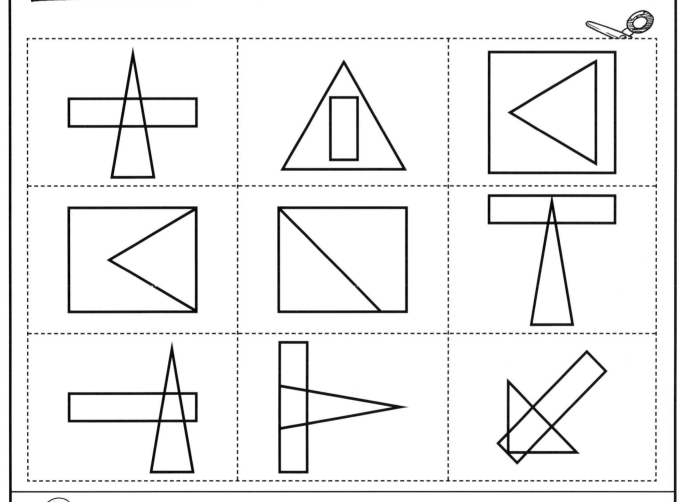

• **Choose three cards. Write descriptions of them so that someone else could pick them from this set.**

Teachers' note Provide one sheet per pair, ideally copied onto card so that the shapes cannot be seen through the paper. As a further extension, encourage the children to talk to each other about the cards and to decide how they would like to sort them into groups. Accept any ways of sorting, encouraging the children to explain their reasoning to others. The cards could be stuck onto separate pieces of paper in their sets and displayed for further discussion.

Developing Numeracy
Using & Applying Maths
Year 4
© A & C BLACK

Be systematic, co-operate and visualise

- **Work with a partner.**

You need a real clock with movable hands and two copies of this sheet.

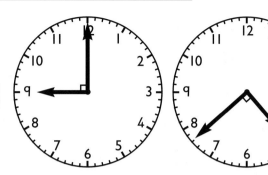

- **Record the times in one day when**

  the hands of a clock are at right angles (90°) to each other.

Teachers' note The children will need real clocks where the hour hand moves in conjunction with the minute hand. If there is an insufficient number of clocks, the children could work in small groups. Ensure they are aware that the hour hand does not stay on the hour number for the whole hour, since this will lead to incorrect answers (for example, quarter past 12 is not a right angle, whereas just after quarter past 12 is). As an extension, the children could write the times in words or in digital form.

Developing Numeracy
Using & Applying Maths
Year 4
© A & C BLACK

Point patterns

A large rectangle is drawn on this grid.

Smaller rectangles have been drawn inside.

- For each rectangle, write the ⟦ co-ordinates ⟧ of its corners (vertices). Start with the largest rectangle.

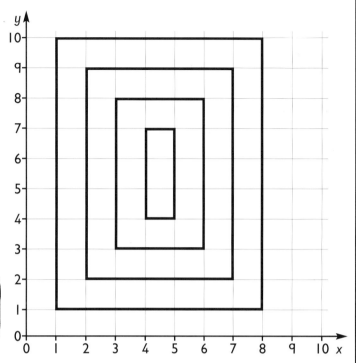

Be careful to write them in the correct column of the table.

	Bottom-left corner	Top-left corner	Bottom-right corner	Top-right corner
Largest	(1 , 1)	(,)	(,)	(,)
	(,)	(,)	(,)	(,)
	(,)	(,)	(,)	(,)
Smallest	(,)	(,)	(,)	(,)

- **Talk to a partner about the patterns in the co-ordinates.**

- **What do you notice about the co-ordinates of corners at the:**

bottom left? _____

top left? _____

bottom right?

_____

- **On squared paper, draw a grid and a different large rectangle. Then draw smaller rectangles inside it.**
- **Are there patterns in the co-ordinates?**

Teachers' note Revise how to write co-ordinates and remind the children that the first co-ordinate shows how many across to move from the origin. A phrase such as 'in the house and up the stairs' can help them to remember this. When the children have completed the table, check their answers before they begin to explore the patterns. Encourage them to try adding the co-ordinates: for example, (8, 1) has the total 9. (See also page 12.) Provide squared paper for the extension activity.

Developing Numeracy
Using & Applying Maths
Year 4
© A & C BLACK

Star gazing

Visualise and generalise

Some shapes can be made into stars, by drawing a longer line along each side of the shape.

Look at this hexagon.

- **Use a ruler to draw longer lines along each side of these shapes. Which ones make stars?**

octagon

triangle

heptagon

pentagon

 Now try this!

- **Try other shapes.**
- **What must be special about them to make stars?**

pentagon

square

Teachers' note There is more than one reason why some shapes result in stars and others do not (see pages 12–13). The children should draw around plastic shapes to take this investigation further. Draw attention to the number of sides, their angles and the relationships between two sides separated by a side, such as the two vertical sides of the last pentagon. The children could explore irregular shapes, different triangles and quadrilaterals, and even those with concave sides.

**Developing Numeracy
Using & Applying Maths
Year 4
© A & C BLACK**

Ribbon predictions

Make predictions, visualise and test your ideas

- **If you fold these** nets **to make cubes, which do you think will have one joined-up piece of ribbon? Put a tick or cross in the ring on each net.**

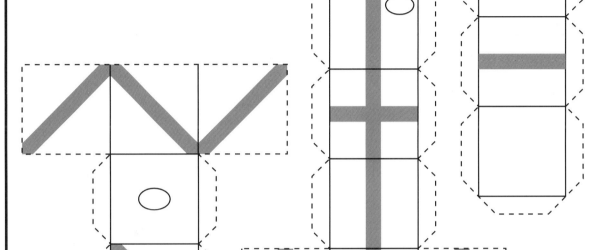

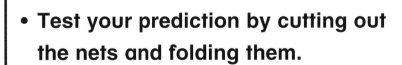

- **Test your prediction by cutting out the nets and folding them.**

- **Draw around a plastic square six times to make a net of a cube. Draw a ribbon puzzle on it for a partner to solve.**

Teachers' note If possible, enlarge this sheet onto thin card or ask the children to glue the sheet of paper onto card. This prediction activity can lead to further investigation of which arrangements of ribbon pieces on a cube net make joined ribbons, and which do not. For the extension activity, provide plastic squares for the children to draw around. More confident children could explore curved ribbons.

**Developing Numeracy
Using & Applying Maths
Year 4
© A & C BLACK**

Starman

☆ In a computer game, a robot must enter a maze and collect **every** star to go on to the next level.

☆ **Without drawing on the maze,** choose a route for the robot. Write instructions for your route so that someone else can follow it.

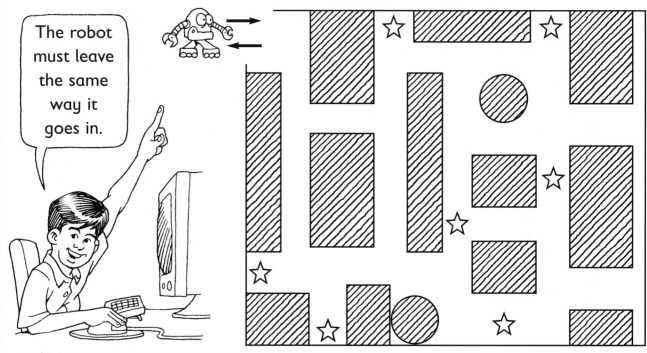

The robot must leave the same way it goes in.

My instructions

• **Swap sheets with a partner. Can you follow each other's routes?**

Teachers' note Since the focus of this activity is on recording, resist the temptation to give examples of how to do this. Instead, the children should try their own methods. Some may give a written description which makes reference to the name and size of the shapes in the maze; others may concentrate on directions (using phrases such as 'turn left', 'turn right', 'go straight on').

Developing Numeracy
Using & Applying Maths
Year 4
© A & C BLACK

Tile tricks: 1

- **Work with a partner.** **You need** the cards cut from *Tile tricks: 2.*

Each tile can be arranged in four ways:

1   2   3   4

- **Arrange the tiles in a 4 × 4 grid to make these patterns.**

  The numbers tell you which way up to put each tile.

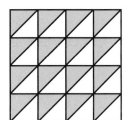

1	1	1	1
1	1	1	1
1	1	1	1
1	1	1	1

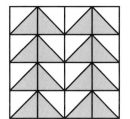

3	4	3	4
3	4	3	4
3	4	3	4
3	4	3	4

- **Make these patterns and write the numbers for them.**

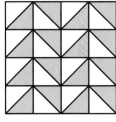

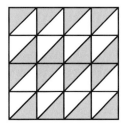

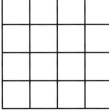

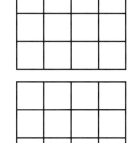

- **Shade the patterns for these numbers.**

2	4	2	4
4	2	4	2
2	4	2	4
4	2	4	2

1	1	1	2
4	3	4	2
4	2	1	2
4	3	3	3

- **On squared paper, make up your own patterns and write the numbers. Then write some numbers first and see what pattern they make!**

Teachers' note Each pair will need a copy of page 46. Provide squared paper for the extension activity. When investigating other patterns that can be created, lead the children to appreciate that using numbers to record the orientation of the tiles is a good way of exploring, recording and quickly comparing patterns.

**Developing Numeracy
Using & Applying Maths
Year 4**
© A & C BLACK

Tile tricks: 2

Visualise, look for patterns and make decisions

• **Carefully cut out these 16 square tiles.**

Teachers' note These tiles should be used with the activity on page 45. Each pair will need one copy of the sheet. The cards could be laminated to create a more permanent resource.

Developing Numeracy
Using & Applying Maths
Year 4
© A & C BLACK

Exercise mats

Five people go to an exercise class in a village hall.

Their five mats fit exactly on the hall floor.

- **Cut out the mats at the bottom of the sheet.**

  Use them to help you draw different ways

  that they can be arranged in the hall.

mat	mat	mat	mat	mat

One way has been drawn for you.

Exercise mats

mat	mat	mat	mat	mat

Teachers' note Encourage the children to compare their solutions and to cross off any that are repeated in order to see how many different arrangements they have found. They should discuss which solutions are rotations of each other, by considering which solutions would look the same if the hall was turned through a half turn.

Developing Numeracy
Using & Applying Maths
Year 4
© A & C BLACK

Spiralling out of control

Make estimates and co-operate

• **Play this game with a partner.**

You need a ruler and some string.

☆ Both players estimate the length of spiral **A** to the nearest half centimetre, for example $12\frac{1}{2}$ cm.

☆ Measure the spiral with string and a ruler to check the estimates. The player who is closer scores a point.

☆ Do the same for spirals **B** to **E**.

☆ The winner is the player with the most points.

A

B

C

D

E

Teachers' note Each pair will need one copy of the sheet, some string and a ruler. Before beginning, demonstrate how to measure the length of a spiral using string and a ruler, and discuss estimating and measuring to the nearest half centimetre. To make a second sheet with spirals of different lengths, the page could be reduced when photocopying (for example, to 96% or 84%).

Developing Numeracy
Using & Applying Maths
Year 4
© A & C BLACK